THE
SECRETS
OF
AS A MAN THINKETH

ADAM MORTIMER
& JAMES ALLEN

PLAIN SIGHT
PUBLISHING
AN IMPRINT OF CEDAR FORT, INC.
SPRINGVILLE, UTAH

Brilliant! Adam Mortimer has uncovered the simple truths of the timeless work As a Man Thinketh *and used down-to-earth explanations and examples to enlighten all who read it. This is a treasure for old and young alike!*

—*Steve Gardner,*
author of Your Superpowers: Dream It! Achieve It!

Adam's commentary on James Allen's thoughts has really brought {As a Man Thinketh] *to life for me. The eloquent and yet archaic language of the book's original form are clarified through Adam's use of modern terminology, and I love the quotes he interjects from famous spiritual teachers! This is inspirational and educational all at the same time!*

—*Janeen J. Detrick,*
owner of Good Vibrations Energy Clinic, LLC

Before reading this book, I applied the law of attraction a few times without realizing what I was doing. This book made it possible to use the law purposefully, opening limitless possibilities that changed my life. Talking about it with Adam lifted my life to an even higher level.

—*Patricia Viette,*
professional photographer, 2011 Gala Award winner

Mind is the Master power that moulds and makes,
And Man is Mind, and evermore he takes
The tool of Thought, and, shaping what he wills,
Brings forth a thousand joys a thousand ills:

He thinks in secret, and it comes to pass:
Environment is but his looking-glass.

James Allen

Some punctuation in *As a Man Thinketh* excerpts has been modernized for clarity and ease of reading.

ISBN: 978-1-4621-1143-5

Published by Plain Sight, an imprint of Cedar Fort, Inc., 2373 W. 700 S., Springville, UT 84663
Distributed by Cedar Fort, Inc., www.cedarfort.com

LIBRARY OF CONGRESS CATALOGING-IN-PUBLICATION DATA

 Mortimer, Adam H., 1981- , author.
The secret of as a man thinketh / Adam H. Mortimer.
pages cm
Summary: Discusses how our thoughts and attitudes influence our successes and failures.
Includes bibliographical references and index.
ISBN 978-1-4621-1143-5 (alk. paper)
1. Positive psychology. 2. Thought and thinking. 3. Success. 4. Peace of mind. I. Title.
BF204.6.M67 2012
158.1--dc23

2012012494

Cover design by Brian Halley
Page design by Erica Dixon
Cover design © 2012 by Lyle Mortimer
Edited by Whitney A. Lindsley

Printed in China

10 9 8 7 6 5 4 3 2 1

Printed on acid-free paper

To my twin boys,
Kenneth and Chandler

Contents

Foreword

This little volume (the result of meditation and experience) is not intended as an exhaustive treatise on the much-written-upon subject of the power of thought. It is suggestive rather than explanatory, its object being to stimulate men and women to the discovery and perception of the truth that

"They themselves are makers of themselves"

by virtue of the thoughts, which they choose and encourage; that mind is the master-weaver, both of the inner garment of character and the outer garment of circumstance, and that, as they may have hitherto woven in ignorance and pain they may now weave in enlightenment and happiness.

I began my journey with As a Man Thinketh *nearly ten years ago. It's a book that I felt compelled to read, yet at the time I did not really know why. The poem that begins "Mind is the master power" was so profound that I memorized it, even though I had not yet fully grasped its meaning. Now I understand, and I have been able to share this secret with thousands of students through my coaching. This book has brought me a new perspective on life.*

"As [a man] thinketh in his heart, so is he."

Proverbs 23:7

Thought
and Character

The aphorism "As a man thinketh in his heart so is he" not only embraces the whole of a man's being but is so comprehensive as to reach out to every condition and circumstance of his life. A man is literally *what he thinks*, his character being the complete sum of all his thoughts.

Have you ever thought that you are the creator of your circumstances? Is everything within you and outside of you a direct result of what you think? Who you are is the sum of every thought that you have had. With honest reflection, you will start to see the truth of this unfolding in your life. As you reflect on past experiences, you will start to see that this golden thread of truth has shaped your reality.

As the plant springs from, and could not be without, the seed, so every act of a man springs from the hidden seeds of thought, and could not have appeared without them. This applies equally to those acts called "spontaneous" and "unpremeditated" as to those which are deliberately executed.

James Allen is teaching the law of the harvest,

> *"For whatsoever a man soweth, that shall he also reap."*
>
> ## Galatians 6:7

Your spontaneous actions were brought into your life with the conscious and unconscious thoughts you have had up to this point.

Act is the blossom of thought, and joy and suffering are its fruits; thus does a man garner in the sweet and bitter fruitage of his own husbandry.

You may or may not see yourself as the creator of your circumstances, but is there harm in imagining that you are? Would that not further purify your thoughts, actions, and everything else that will help you to accomplish your desired life goals?

"Thought in the mind hath made us, What we are
By thought was wrought and built. If a man's mind
Hath evil thoughts, pain comes on him as comes
The wheel the ox behind. . . .

God has given us the power to create. Our thoughts and the power of our imagination allow us to create what we will. But be mindful of your thoughts. Just like the law of gravity does not deviate, the laws of the mind are true and unchanging. Your environment by universal law must reflect your thoughts. Everything outside of you mirrors what is inside of you. Jesus taught not to worry about the mote in your brother's eye when you have a beam in your own. Indeed, you notice the mote in your brother's eye because it is a reflection of your own thoughts.

. . . If one endure
In purity of thought, joy follows him
As his own shadow—sure."

What a wonderful thought. As you clean your mind, joy will follow you, even as surely as your own shadow.

Man is a growth by law, and not a creation by artifice, and cause and effect is as absolute and undeviating in the hidden realm of thought as in the world of visible and material things. A noble and Godlike character is not a thing of favour or chance, but is the natural result of continued effort in right thinking, the effect of long-cherished association with Godlike thoughts. An ignoble and bestial character, by the same process, is the result of the continued harbouring of grovelling thoughts.

Good people are not good by chance. If people are good and positive, it is because they have created that habit of thought.

Maxwell Maltz once said, "Happiness is a habit of thought." It stands to reason that the alternative is true as well.

> *"Most people are about as happy as they make up their minds to be."*
>
> Abraham Lincoln

Man is made or unmade by himself; in the armoury of thought he forges the weapons by which he destroys himself; he also fashions the tools with which he builds for himself heavenly mansions of joy and strength and peace. By the right choice and true application of thought, man ascends to the Divine Perfection; by the abuse and wrong application of thought, he descends below the level of the beast. Between these two extremes are all the grades of character, and man is their maker and master.

Of all the beautiful truths pertaining to the soul which have been restored and brought to light in this age, none is more gladdening or fruitful of divine promise and confidence than this—that man is the master of thought, the moulder of character, and the maker and shaper of condition, environment, and destiny.

God has truly blessed man with one of his greatest attributes: the power to create. We create every aspect of our lives. We create the world that we want to live in through our consistent thoughts. Heaven stands ready to assist the man who will use these powers constructively. Is it not written, "Ask and ye shall receive?" In my line of work, I have the opportunity counsel with many people about their financial situations. To help them, I often quote the following poem:

> I bargained with Life for a penny,
> And Life would pay no more,
> However I begged at evening
> When I counted my scanty store;
> For Life is a just employer,
> He gives you what you ask,
> But once you have set the wages,
> Why, you must bear the task.
> I worked for a menial's hire,
> Only to learn, dismayed,
> That any wage I had asked of Life,
> Life would have paid.
>
> ## Jessie Belle Rittenhouse

After I quote this to my students, I often ask, "What have you specifically asked of life when it comes to money?" The most common responses are "Nothing" or "To get by." And as these students reflect on their lives, they prove to themselves the validity of the poem, for they have received exactly what they have asked for, and not a penny more.

As a being of Power, Intelligence, and Love, and the lord of his own thoughts, man holds the key to every situation, and contains within himself that transforming and regenerative agency by which he may make himself what he wills.

Man is always the master, even in his weaker and most abandoned state; but in his weakness and degradation he is the foolish master who misgoverns his "household." When he begins to reflect upon his condition, and to search diligently for the Law upon which his being is established, he then becomes the wise master, directing his energies with intelligence and fashioning his thoughts to fruitful issues. Such is the *conscious* master, and man can only thus become by discovering *within himself* the laws of thought; which discovery is totally a matter of application, self-analysis, and experience.

I hope that by using this book, you may discover that you are the master of your life. When you find yourself at a low point, remember to lift your circumstances. You must first lift your thoughts; then, by universal law, your circumstances must change. Breaking the cycle of negative thinking can be a bit challenging. I am a big believer in having a coach. A coach operates in a separate belief system and therefore can point out the beliefs that may be limiting you. Once you have discovered a limiting belief, which is often subconscious, you must learn to clear old beliefs to make room for those that are new and more empowering.

A limiting belief is any belief that in any way holds you back from achieving goals. Remember that God does not want his children to limit themselves.

> *"With God all things are possible."*
>
> Matthew 19:26

Only by much searching and mining are gold and diamonds obtained, and man can find every truth connected with his being, if he will dig deep into the mine of his soul; and that he is the maker of his character, the molder of his life, and the builder of his destiny, he may unerringly prove, if he will watch, control, and alter his thoughts, tracing their effects upon himself, upon others, and upon his life and circumstances, linking cause and effect by patient practice and investigation, and utilizing his every experience, even to the most trivial, everyday occurrence, as a means of obtaining that knowledge of himself which is Understanding, Wisdom, Power. In this direction, as in no other, is the law absolute that "He that seeketh findeth; and to him that knocketh it shall be opened;" for only by patience, practice, and ceaseless importunity can a man enter the Door of the Temple of Knowledge.

Many people have heard of these things, and because they have heard of them, they think they understand them. People say, "I get it. I understand how this all works." My response to them is that if you are not living the life of your dreams, then you do not get it. You must want it so badly that you are willing to make the necessary sacrifices of time and energy to uncover this secret.

Effect of Thought on Circumstances

Man's mind may be likened to a garden, which may be intelligently cultivated or allowed to run wild; but whether cultivated or neglected, it must, and will, *bring forth*. If no useful seeds are *put* into it, then an abundance of useless weed-seeds will *fall* therein, and will continue to produce their kind.

Just as a gardener cultivates his plot, keeping it free from weeds, and growing the flowers and fruits which he requires, so may a man tend the garden of his mind, weeding out all the wrong, useless, and impure thoughts, and cultivating toward perfection the flowers and fruits of right, useful, and pure thoughts. By pursuing this process, a man sooner or later discovers that he is the master-gardener of his soul, the director of his life. He also reveals, within himself, the laws of thought, and understands, with ever-increasing accuracy, how the thought-forces and mind elements operate in the shaping of his character, circumstances, and destiny.

There are two types of beliefs: conscious and subconscious. Most people can easily discover their conscious limiting beliefs, but it takes some deeper thinking and reflection to discover those that are subconscious. Many people do not realize that they are living through their parents' belief systems. Your parents may have accepted their beliefs from their parents and passed them on to you. These beliefs may be centuries old. Take, for example, one man who was perplexed about his financial situation. There seemed to be a force that was preventing him from achieving his financial goals. Every time he tried to improve his financial situation, something always came up. We later found that he had adopted his father's belief system about money. His father lived in the scarcity mind-set, and his environment inevitably reflected his mentality. Once this student became conscious of the subconscious, he was able to choose a new belief and make significantly more money.

Thought and character are one, and as character can only manifest and discover itself through environment and circumstance, the outer conditions of a person's life will always be found to be harmoniously related to his inner state. This does not mean that a man's circumstances at any given time are an indication of his *entire* character, but that those circumstances are so intimately connected with some vital thought-element within himself that, for the time being, they are indispensable to his development.

Every man is where he is by the law of his being; the thoughts which he has built into his character have brought him there, and in the arrangement of his life there is no element of chance, but all is the result of a law which cannot err. This is just as true of those who feel "out of harmony" with their surroundings as of those who are contented with them.

Are you in harmony with your environment? This will reveal to you the beliefs within you that are empowering and disempowering.

As a progressive and evolving being, man is where he is that he may learn that he may grow; and as he learns the spiritual lesson which any circumstance contains for him, it passes away and gives place to other circumstances.

Once you learn the lessons, you no longer need the experience. Accepting that you are totally responsible for where you are in life is a great step toward personal development. It may not be the most comfortable thing to do, but the honest and humble of heart will learn this spiritual lesson and continually grow.

Man is buffeted by circumstances so long as he believes himself to be the creature of outside conditions, but when he realizes that he is a creative power, and that he may command the hidden soil and seeds of his being out of which circumstances grow, he then becomes the rightful master of himself.

"[Man] may command the hidden soil and seeds of his being out of which circumstances grow." This is one of the most powerful God-given gifts, to prosper in any circumstance. The unsuccessful person is a slave to circumstance, while the successful person controls his circumstances. True empowerment comes from knowing that you are in control of your life and your destiny.

That circumstances grow out of thought every man knows who has for any length of time practised self-control and self-purification, for he will have noticed that the alteration in his circumstances has been in exact ratio with his altered mental condition. So true is this that when a man earnestly applies himself to remedy the defects in his character, and makes swift and marked progress, he passes rapidly through a succession of vicissitudes.

Think back on a time in your life when you have worked on becoming a better person. Think of your circumstances during those times. Did your circumstances line up with your thoughts? Think of when your thoughts have been disempowering and notice how your circumstances lined up with that way of thinking as well.

The soul attracts that which it secretly harbours; that which it loves, and also that which it fears; it reaches the height of its cherished aspirations; it falls to the level of its unchastened desires—and circumstances are the means by which the soul receives its own.

You can discover what you are bringing into your life by tuning in to your emotions. Your emotions will reveal what you truly believe subconsciously and will activate the unseen forces that bring what you desire into existence. What are the thoughts that you consistently dwell on and mix with emotion? Are they visions of fear and worry, or are they visions of belief and faith? The beliefs that have the strongest emotions attached to them, whether positive or negative, are on their way into your life.

Every thought-seed sown or allowed to fall into the mind, and to take root there, produces its own, blossoming sooner or later into act, and bearing its own fruitage of opportunity and circumstance. Good thoughts bear good fruit, bad thoughts bad fruit.

This is a great universal law. The seeds of thought that you put in your mind must unequivocally come back to you, including your actions. Actions speak more to who you are than anything you may say. Your actions show the world your true thoughts.

> *"Ye shall know them by their fruits."*
>
> Matthew 7:16

The outer world of circumstance shapes itself to the inner world of thought, and both pleasant and unpleasant external conditions are factors, which make for the ultimate good of the individual. As the reaper of his own harvest, man learns both by suffering and bliss.

There was once a man who needed a roof for his temple. He searched and searched for someone who would qualify for the job. There simply were no roofers around. All he found was a man who knew how to build ships. He thought to himself, If this man can build a watertight ship, then why not a watertight roof? Do not the same principles in building a ship apply to building a roof? He concluded that a roof is really just a ship upside down. We often learn more from our failures than our successes. If you have circumstances that you do not want in your life, turn your ship upside down.

Following the inmost desires, aspirations, thoughts, by which he allows himself to be dominated, (pursuing the will-o'-the-wisps of impure imaginings or steadfastly walking the highway of strong and high endeavor), a man at last arrives at their fruition and fulfillment in the outer conditions of his life. The laws of growth and adjustment everywhere obtains.

A man does not come to the almshouse or the jail by the tyranny of fate or circumstance but by the pathway of grovelling thoughts and base desires. Nor does a pure-minded man fall suddenly into crime by stress of any mere external force; the criminal thought had long been secretly fostered in the heart, and the hour of opportunity revealed its gathered power. Circumstance does not make the man; it reveals him to himself. No such conditions can exist as descending into vice and its attendant sufferings apart from vicious inclinations, or ascending into virtue and its pure happiness without the continued cultivation of virtuous aspirations; and man, therefore, as the lord and master of thought, is the maker of himself, the shaper and author of environment. Even at birth the soul comes to its own and through every step of its earthly pilgrimage it attracts those combinations of conditions which reveal itself, which are the reflections of its own purity and impurity, its strength and weakness.

"Thoughts are things."

Napoleon Hill

Men do not attract that which they *want*, but that which they *are*. Their whims, fancies, and ambitions are thwarted at every step, but their inmost thoughts and desires are fed with their own food, be it foul or clean. The "divinity that shapes our ends" is in ourselves; it is our very self. Only himself manacles man: thought and action are the gaolers of Fate—they imprison, being base; they are also the angels of Freedom—they liberate, being noble. Not what he wishes and prays for does a man get, but what he justly earns. His wishes and prayers are only gratified and answered when they harmonize with his thoughts and actions.

How can we use this knowledge to get what we want in life? We must embody the things we desire. If you want to have more spirituality in your environment, you must become spiritual. If you want more abundance, you must first become that way in the mind. If you want better health, then you must first become whole in the mind. You may be saying to yourself, "How can I do this? How can I act that way when that is not who I am yet?" As the saying goes, "Fake it till you make it." In other words, act as if you are that person until it becomes a habit of thought.

The story of the man who found an extra four thousand dollars a month illustrates this quite beautifully. I will call this man Jared. Jared wanted to be wealthy. He wanted to generate extra income and to eliminate all of his debts as quickly as possible.

His current belief system blinded him to money-making opportunities. All he could see at the end of the month was four hundred dollars left over to use to implement his debt-elimination plan. He was talking to his wise friend about his goals and about the fact that his plans were moving painfully slow.

This friend asked him, "Why not do four thousand dollars a month toward paying off your debts?" This was a big shock to Jared's current beliefs, and he looked at his friend as if he were crazy. This friend invited him to believe in the unbelievable. He told Jared to suspend all disbelief for at least three weeks. Jared agreed to this, and what happened next seemed like magic. Money-making ideas began to flood Jared's mind. Within twelve weeks, Jared had found a way to accomplish his goal.

In the light of this truth, what, then, is the meaning of "fighting against circumstances?" It means that a man is continually revolting against an *effect* without, while all the time he is nourishing and preserving its *cause* in his heart. That cause may take the form of a conscious vice or an unconscious weakness; but whatever it is, it stubbornly retards the efforts of its possessor, and thus calls aloud for remedy.

Trying to change the outside world without changing the inside is like trying to pump up a tire by blowing air around it and not into it. You must focus on the root cause of the problem and not just its effects.

Men are anxious to improve their circumstances, but are unwilling to improve themselves; they therefore remain bound. The man who does not shrink from self-crucifixion can never fail to accomplish the object upon which his heart is set. This is as true of earthly as of heavenly things. Even the man whose sole object is to acquire wealth must be prepared to make great personal sacrifices before he can accomplish his object; and how much more so he who would realize a strong and well-poised life?

If I were to walk into a classroom and ask the class, "Who here desires prosperity?," the students would all raise their hands. If I were to ask, "Who is willing to track their expenses and their net worth every day?"; "Who is willing to live on a budget?"; or "Who is willing to cultivate the millionaire mentality?," little by little, hands would begin to drop. Many desire success in life, but few are willing to sacrifice what is necessary to make it a reality.

Here is a man who is wretchedly poor. He is extremely anxious that his surroundings and home comforts should be improved, yet all the time he shirks his work, and considers he is justified in trying to deceive his employer on the ground of the insufficiency of his wages. Such a man does not understand the simplest rudiments of those principles which are the basis of true prosperity, and is not only totally unfitted to rise out of his wretchedness, but is actually attracting to himself a still deeper wretchedness by dwelling in, and acting out, indolent, deceptive, and unmanly thoughts.

Without being brutally honest with yourself, there can be no progress. Personal growth requires taking personal responsibility.

Here is a rich man who is the victim of a painful and persistent disease as the result of gluttony. He is willing to give large sums of money to get rid of it, but he will not sacrifice his gluttonous desires. He wants to gratify his taste for rich and unnatural viands and have his health as well. Such a man is totally unfit to have health, because he has not yet learned the first principles of a healthy life.

Here is an employer of labour who adopts crooked measures to avoid paying the regulation wage, and, in the hope of making larger profits, reduces the wages of his workpeople. Such a man is altogether unfitted for prosperity, and when he finds himself bankrupt, both as regards reputation and riches, he blames circumstances, not knowing that he is the sole author of his condition.

I have introduced these three cases merely as illustrative of the truth that man is the causer (though nearly always is [so] unconsciously) of his circumstances, and that, whilst aiming at a good end, he is continually frustrating its accomplishment by encouraging thoughts and desires which cannot possibly harmonize with that end. Such cases could be multiplied and varied almost indefinitely, but this is not necessary, as the reader can, if he so resolves, trace the action of the laws of thought in his own mind and life, and until this is done, mere external facts cannot serve as a ground of reasoning.

Circumstances, however, are so complicated, thought is so deeply rooted, and the conditions of happiness vary so vastly with individuals, that a man's entire soul-condition (although it may be known to himself) cannot be judged by another from the external aspect of his life alone. A man may be honest in certain directions, yet suffer privations; a man may be dishonest in certain directions, yet acquire wealth; but the conclusion usually formed that the one man fails because of his particular honesty, and that the other prospers because of his particular dishonesty, is the result of a superficial judgment, which assumes that the dishonest man is almost totally corrupt, and the honest man almost entirely virtuous. In the light of a deeper knowledge and wider experience such judgment is found to be erroneous. The dishonest man may have some admirable virtues, which the other does not possess; and the honest man obnoxious vices which are absent in the other. The honest man reaps the good results of his honest thoughts and acts; he also brings upon himself the sufferings which his vices produce. The dishonest man likewise garners his own suffering and happiness.

We tend to simplify the cause and effect of circumstances when judging the lives of others. We cannot justly judge one another because we do not know all the complexities of the thoughts that have brought them to their circumstances. We cannot assume the character of a person because that person is rich or poor. There is so much more to it. As James states, there may be good qualities in one and vices in the other that we may not be aware of.

It is pleasing to human vanity to believe that one suffers because of one's virtue; but not until a man has extirpated every sickly, bitter, and impure thought from his mind, and washed every sinful stain from his soul, can he be in a position to know and declare that his sufferings are the result of his good, and not of his bad qualities; and on the way to, yet long before he has reached, that supreme perfection, he will have found, working in his mind and life, the Great Law which is absolutely just, and which cannot, therefore, give good for evil, evil for good. Possessed of such knowledge, he will then know, looking back upon his past ignorance and blindness, that his life is, and always was, justly ordered, and that all his past experiences, good and bad, were the equitable outworking of his evolving, yet unevolved self.

Good thoughts and actions can never produce bad results; bad thoughts and actions can never produce good results. This is but saying that nothing can come from corn but corn, nothing from nettles but nettles. Men understand this law in the natural world, and work with it; but few understand it in the mental and moral world (though its operation there is just as simple and undeviating), and they, therefore, do not cooperate with it.

Suffering cannot and will not come from good thinking. It would go against the law of the harvest. What you send out there must come back to you. There is an order to the universe and there are laws that cannot be broken.

Suffering is *always* the effect of wrong thought in some direction. It is an indication that the individual is out of harmony with himself, with the Law of his being. The sole and supreme use of suffering is to purify, to burn out all that is useless and impure. Suffering ceases for him who is pure. There could be no object in burning gold after the dross had been removed, and a perfectly pure and enlightened being could not suffer.

The circumstances which a man encounters with suffering are the result of his own mental inharmony. The circumstances which a man encounters with blessedness are the result of his own mental harmony. Blessedness, not material possessions, is the measure of right thought; wretchedness, not lack of material possessions, is the measure of wrong thought. A man may be cursed and rich; he may be blessed and poor. Blessedness and riches are only joined together when the riches are rightly and wisely used; and the poor man only descends into wretchedness when he regards his lot as a burden unjustly imposed.

Indigence and indulgence are the two extremes of wretchedness. They are both equally unnatural and the result of mental disorder. A man is not rightly conditioned until he is a happy, healthy, and prosperous being; and happiness, health, and prosperity are the result of a harmonious adjustment of the inner with the outer, of the man with his surroundings.

A man only begins to be a man when he ceases to whine and revile, and commences to search for the hidden justice which regulates his life. And as he adapts his mind to that regulating factor, he ceases to accuse others as the cause of his condition, and builds himself up in strong and noble thoughts; ceases to kick against circumstances, but begins to use them as aids to his more rapid progress, and as a means of discovering the hidden powers and possibilities within himself.

A sign of maturity is taking responsibility for your life experience. This means that you must not place blame on others or live as a victim. When you choose to do something about your environment, you are in a new state of empowerment.

Law, not confusion, is the dominating principle in the universe; justice, not injustice, is the soul and substance of life; and righteousness, not corruption, is the moulding and moving force in the spiritual government of the world. This being so, man has but to right himself to find that the universe is right; and during the process of putting himself right he will find that as he alters his thoughts toward things and other people, things and other people will alter toward him.

God is a god of order. There are natural laws, and there are spiritual laws. These laws are in full force whether you accept it or not. Once you understand these laws, you can use them to your benefit. Just like a basic understanding of the law of gravity helps man to fly, knowing these laws of the mind will allow you to live your life without limits.

> "Anything the mind of man can conceive and believe it can achieve."
>
> Napoleon Hill

The proof of this truth is in every person, and it therefore admits of easy investigation by systematic introspection and self-analysis. Let a man radically alter his thoughts, and he will be astonished at the rapid transformation it will effect in the material conditions of his life. Men imagine that thought can be kept secret, but it cannot; it rapidly crystallizes into habit, and habit solidifies into circumstance. Bestial thoughts crystallize into habits of drunkenness and sensuality, which solidify into circumstances of destitution and disease: impure thoughts of every kind crystallize into enervating and confusing habits, which solidify into distracting and adverse circumstances: thoughts of fear, doubt, and indecision crystallize into weak, unmanly, and irresolute habits, which solidify into circumstances of failure, indigence, and slavish dependence; lazy thoughts crystallize into habits of uncleanliness and dishonesty, which solidify into circumstances of foulness and beggary; hateful and condemnatory thoughts crystallize into habits of accusation and violence, which solidify into circumstances of injury and persecution; selfish thoughts of all kinds crystallize into habits of self-seeking, which solidify into circumstances more or less distressing. On the other hand, beautiful thoughts of all kinds crystallize into habits of grace and kindliness, which solidify into genial and sunny circumstances; pure thoughts crystallize into habits of temperance and self-control, which solidify into circumstances of repose and peace: thoughts of courage, self-reliance, and decision crystallize into manly habits, which solidify into circumstances of success, plenty, and freedom; energetic thoughts crystallize into habits of cleanliness and industry, which solidify into circumstances of pleasantness; gentle and forgiving thoughts crystallize into habits of gentleness, which solidify into protective and preservative circumstances; loving and unselfish thoughts crystallize into habits of self-forgetfulness for others, which solidify into circumstances of sure and abiding prosperity and true riches.

I am amazed at the people that have miraculously altered what they thought was their lot in their lives simply by altering their thoughts. In as little as thirty days, you can alter your internal belief system. Choose a new circumstance that you would like to have. Suspend all your disbelief in what you would like to see happen in your life. Spend your time visualizing, feeling, and acting as if you are already in possession of what you would like to have. Believe it to the point that there is no doubt in your mind. This point is called "the knowing," when you just know that this is going to happen. Listen to the inspiration that you receive—it will guide you to the fulfillment of your desires. Do this for three to four weeks. You can also state affirmations that align with the goal that you would like to receive.

A few examples of money-making affirmations are as follows:

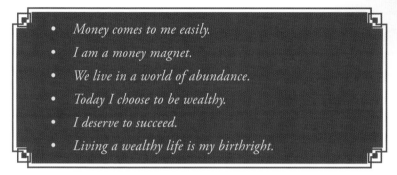

- *Money comes to me easily.*
- *I am a money magnet.*
- *We live in a world of abundance.*
- *Today I choose to be wealthy.*
- *I deserve to succeed.*
- *Living a wealthy life is my birthright.*

A particular train of thought persisted in, be it good or bad, cannot fail to produce its results on the character and circumstances. A man cannot directly choose his circumstances, but he can choose his thoughts, and so indirectly, yet surely, shape his circumstances.

This was once explained to me by a spiritual leader. He said, "You can choose one end of the stick that you pick up, but once you have picked up one end, you cannot choose the other end." Once you have made a choice, it will come to pass. Choose wisely, for your choice will manifest itself through circumstances.

Nature helps every man to the gratification of the thoughts, which he most encourages, and opportunities are presented which will most speedily bring to the surface both the good and evil thoughts.

This miraculous force will bring the right types of people and resources in the fulfillment of your most sincere desires. The universe will align itself to bring what it is you most desire into your life as quickly and as efficiently as possible.

Let a man cease from his sinful thoughts, and all the world will soften toward him, and be ready to help him; let him put away his weakly and sickly thoughts, and lo, opportunities will spring up on every hand to aid his strong resolves; let him encourage good thoughts, and no hard fate shall bind him down to wretchedness and shame. The world is your kaleidoscope, and the varying combinations of colours, which at every succeeding moment it presents to you are the exquisitely adjusted pictures of your ever-moving thoughts.

If you change your thoughts, then you can change your world. Your environment will magically change to align with your new thoughts! Hold on to your dream and believe in it. Does that mean that once you have held a thought in your mind, you can sit back and do nothing? Absolutely not! You must take action to accomplish anything. Once your thoughts are aligned with your desired circumstances, your actions will naturally change. As your actions change, so too do your circumstances.

So You will be what you will to be;
Let failure find its false content
In that poor word, "environment,"
But spirit scorns it, and is free.

It masters time, it conquers space;
It cowes that boastful trickster, Chance,
And bids the tyrant Circumstance
Uncrown, and fill a servant's place.

The human Will, that force unseen,
The offspring of a deathless Soul,
Can hew a way to any goal,
Though walls of granite intervene.

Be not impatient in delays
But wait as one who understands;
When spirit rises and commands
The gods are ready to obey.

James Allen

Effect of Thought on Health and the Body

The body is the servant of the mind. It obeys the operations of the mind, whether they be deliberately chosen or automatically expressed. At the bidding of unlawful thoughts the body sinks rapidly into disease and decay; at the command of glad and beautiful thoughts it becomes clothed with youthfulness and beauty.

Your thoughts are manifested in your health. The body, being the servant to your mind, awaits your commands through what you say, visualize, and feel. Many people worry and have a heart filled with fear and doubt. They weaken their immune systems with these thoughts, and they are bound to get sick. Circumstances must align with what you are thinking even when it comes to your health. Remember, disease is really "dis-ease."

Disease and health, like circumstances, are rooted in thought. Sickly thoughts will express themselves through a sickly body. Thoughts of fear have been known to kill a man as speedily as a bullet, and they are continually killing thousands of people just as surely though less rapidly. The people who live in fear of disease are the people who get it. Anxiety quickly demoralizes the whole body, and lays it open to the entrance of disease; while impure thoughts, even if not physically indulged, will soon shatter the nervous system.

Thoughts based on faith will always produce a strong body, while thoughts rooted in fear will always cause sickness.

Strong, pure, and happy thoughts build up the body in vigour and grace. The body is a delicate and plastic instrument, which responds readily to the thoughts by which it is impressed, and habits of thought will produce their own effects, good or bad, upon it.

It amazes me how many people have not yet discovered the intimate link between thoughts and health. Science is finally catching up to James Allen over a hundred years after this book was written. Through epigenetics, scientists are starting to realize that gene expression can be turned off and on through thoughts.

Men will continue to have impure and poisoned blood so long as they propagate unclean thoughts. Out of a clean heart comes a clean life and a clean body. Out of a defiled mind proceeds a defiled life and a corrupt body. Thought is the fount of action, life, and manifestation; make the fountain pure, and all will be pure.

This is the old "garbage in and garbage out" adage. If you put garbage into your body through your thoughts, then out come garbage words and garbage emotions in the form of fear, stress, and doubt.

Change of diet will not help a man who will not change his thoughts. When a man makes his thoughts pure, he no longer desires impure food.

Did you know that you can actually speed up and slow down your metabolism with your mind? If more people knew this, it would put a whole new spin on weight loss. Half of your work-out program would be thinking, and the other half would be doing. When the practice of great thoughts is mixed with action, miraculous things happen.

Clean thoughts make clean habits. The so-called saint who does not wash his body is not a saint. He who has strengthened and purified his thoughts does not need to consider the malevolent microbe.

If you would protect your body, guard your mind. If you would renew your body, beautify your mind. Thoughts of malice, envy, disappointment, and despondency rob the body of its health and grace. A sour face does not come by chance; it is made by sour thoughts. Wrinkles that mar are drawn by folly, passion, and pride.

Helen "Lady" Solomon Kamana, my wife's great-grandmother, is 103 years old, and she is beautiful. She has refined her body and mind with her thoughts. She has a recipe for longevity, and it is as follows:

- *Praise Jesus*
- *Greet the Day with Cheer*
- *Put a Smile on Your Face*

- *Be in Touch with Family*
- *If You Do Not Have Something Nice to Say, Don't Say Anything*
- *Go to Work with a Good Spirit*
- *No Time for Idleness*

Praise for a higher power brings vitality to the mind. Starting the day with a good attitude typically leads to having a good, full day. You have a few moments after waking up to determine what kind of day it is going to be. After those few moments, the mind will typically fulfill what you have been dwelling on. When you wake up in the morning, your mind is more relaxed than it is at other times of the day, and when the mind is relaxed, the portals of the subconscious are open. Therefore, it is important to start out your day with the correct thoughts. You are literally influencing the subconscious. The same is true when you go to sleep at night.

Your family members are who you will see the most of in your life. If you have a good relationship with your family, don't you have a higher probability of thinking good, life-giving thoughts?

When you go to work, what kind of thoughts do you think? If what you feel and think create your circumstances, is it any wonder that people who love their jobs find themselves in comfortable circumstances?

Keeping busy keeps the mind healthy. Your mind is a goal-striving machine. It is never dormant and is always working toward the fulfilling of your desires. Psychologists have prescribed changing the speed that you walk, the way that you sit, and your body posture for curing depression. The idea is that if the body is doing it, the mind must be thinking it. Walking around as if you are more happy and confident really does work. Try it for a while and watch what happens.

I know a woman of ninety-six who has the bright, innocent face of a girl. I know a man well under middle age whose face is drawn into inharmonious contours. The one is the result of a sweet and sunny disposition; the other is the outcome of passion and discontent.

As you cannot have a sweet and wholesome abode unless you admit the air and sunshine freely into your rooms, so a strong body and a bright, happy, or serene countenance can only result from the free admittance into the mind of thoughts of joy and goodwill and serenity.

On the faces of the aged there are wrinkles made by sympathy, others by strong and pure thought, and others are carved by passion: who cannot distinguish them? With those who have lived righteously, age is calm, peaceful, and softly mellowed, like the setting sun. I have recently seen a philosopher on his deathbed. He was not old except in years. He died as sweetly and peacefully as he had lived.

I believe that one of the greatest blessings in life is to move on from this life peacefully and gracefully. Death does not need to be the monster that the movies have made it out to be. It truly can be a thing of beauty. The peace that you have moving on will be directly correlated to the faith and belief that you have developed in this life.

There is no physician like cheerful thought for dissipating the ills of the body; there is no comforter to compare with goodwill for dispersing the shadows of grief and sorrow. To live continually in thoughts of ill will, cynicism, suspicion, and envy, is to be confined in a self-made prison-hole. But to think well of all, to be cheerful with all, to patiently learn to find the good in all—such unselfish thoughts are the very portals of heaven; and to dwell day by day in thoughts of peace toward every creature will bring abounding peace to their possessor.

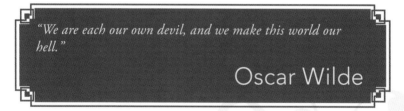 *James Allen is telling us a choice we all have to make. We can be positive and be free of the psychological chains that are holding so many people down, or we can persist in negative thoughts and create a hell of our own making. The choice is ours to make.*

> *"We are each our own devil, and we make this world our hell."*
>
> Oscar Wilde

Thought and Purpose

Until thought is linked with purpose there is no intelligent accomplishment. With the majority the bark of thought is allowed to "drift" upon the ocean of life. Aimlessness is a vice, and such drifting must not continue for him who would steer clear of catastrophe and destruction.

Death follows the aimless wanderer. Life and achievement follow the man that lives his life with passion and vision.

"Where there is no vision, the people perish."

Proverbs 29:18

They who have no central purpose in their life fall an easy prey to petty worries, fears, troubles, and self-pityings, all of which are indications of weakness, which lead, just as surely as deliberately planned sins (though by a different route), to failure, unhappiness, and loss, for weakness cannot persist in a power-evolving universe.

I remember a story told to me by a WWII pilot. When the pilots were on a mission, they would have to fly through flak, which were essentially rockets that would fly up to the level of the planes, explode, and spray shrapnel everywhere. This pilot, after completing many successful runs, was asked what the secret to his success was. He smiled and said, "I stay focused on where I am headed, while the other pilots get distracted by the flak." The secret is that you will fly in the direction you are looking!

A man should conceive of a legitimate purpose in his heart, and set out to accomplish it. He should make this purpose the centralizing point of his thoughts. It may take the form of a spiritual ideal, or it may be a worldly object, according to his nature at the time being; but whichever it is, he should steadily focus his thought-forces upon the object which he has set before him. He should make this purpose his supreme duty, and should devote himself to its attainment, not allowing his thoughts to wander away into ephemeral fancies, longings, and imaginings. This is the royal road to self-control and true concentration of thought. Even if he fails again and again to accomplish his purpose (as he necessarily must until weakness is overcome), the *strength of character gained* will be the measure of his true success, and this will form a new starting-point for future power and triumph.

Purifying your thoughts is a journey. You will not be perfect; in fact, you may fail many times before you reach your final destination. My mentor once gave me a powerful formula for success:

Success = Persistence + Failure

He went on to say that all successful people are persistent failures. When you look at it this way, you realize that failure is an important part of success.

Those who are not prepared for the apprehension of a *great* purpose should fix their thoughts upon the faultless performance of their duty, no matter how insignificant their task may appear. Only in this way can the thoughts be gathered and focused, and resolution and energy be developed, which being done, there is nothing which may not be accomplished.

The weakest soul, knowing its own weakness, and believing this truth *that strength can only be developed by effort and practice*, will, thus believing, at once begin to exert itself, and, adding effort to effort, patience to patience, and strength to strength, will never cease to develop, and will at last grow divinely strong.

Be patient. You cannot tell a flower to grow faster than is natural. Likewise, there are spiritual laws of growth. Be persistent and work hard, and great things will happen. You simply trust the process.

As the physically weak man can make himself strong by careful and patient training, so the man of weak thoughts can make them strong by exercising himself in right thinking.

To put away aimlessness and weakness, and to begin to think with purpose, is to enter the ranks of those strong ones who only recognize failure as one of the pathways to attainment; who make all conditions serve them, and who think strongly, attempt fearlessly, and accomplish masterfully.

Having conceived of his purpose, a man should mentally mark out a *straight* pathway to its achievement, looking neither to the right nor the left. Doubts and fears should be rigorously excluded; they are disintegrating elements, which break up the straight line of effort, rendering it crooked, ineffectual, useless. Thoughts of doubt and fear never accomplished anything, and never can. They always lead to failure. Purpose, energy, power to do, and all strong thoughts cease when doubt and fear creep in.

The will to do springs from the knowledge that we *can* do. Doubt and fear are the great enemies of knowledge, and he who encourages them, who does not slay them, thwarts himself at every step.

> *"Many of us crucify ourselves between two thieves—regret for the past and fear of the future."*
>
> Fulton Oursler

Too many people do not get started because they are thinking "out of the moment" thoughts, those that focus on the past or the future. When do you know that you are out of the moment? The exact moment you say, "I have so much to do." If you are in the moment, you cannot get overwhelmed. In this moment, you only have one thing to do. You can never get overwhelmed if you are living your life in the present.

He who has conquered doubt and fear has conquered failure. His every thought is allied with power, and all difficulties are bravely met and wisely overcome. His purposes are seasonably planted, and they bloom and bring forth fruit, which does not fall prematurely to the ground.

Fear of failure is a real thing for many people. The only way to overcome this is to feel the fear and do it anyway. If we consistently do what we are afraid of, the fear will inevitably go away.

Thought allied fearlessly to purpose becomes creative force: he who *knows* this is ready to become something higher and stronger than a mere bundle of wavering thoughts and fluctuating sensations; he who *does* this has become the conscious and intelligent wielder of his mental powers.

The Thought Factor in Achievement

All that a man achieves and all that he fails to achieve is the direct result of his own thoughts. In a justly ordered universe, where loss of equipoise would mean total destruction, individual responsibility must be absolute. A man's weakness and strength, purity and impurity, are his own and not another man's; they are brought about by himself and not by another; and they can only be altered by himself, never by another. His condition is also his own and not another man's. His suffering and his happiness are evolved from within. As he thinks, so he is; as he continues to think, so he remains.

Recently people have been complaining about the economy and how it has caused all of their problems. However, their thoughts, not the economy have caused their suffering. As my mentor once put it, "The economy may be suffering, but your own personal economy may be thriving." Do not buy into the down mind-set of a down economy if you do not want that reflected in your own situation.

A strong man cannot help a weaker unless that weaker is *willing* to be helped, and even then the weak man must become strong of himself; he must, by his own efforts, develop the strength which he admires in another. None but himself can alter his condition.

Change comes from within.

Each person must learn, struggle, and grow independently. Someone cannot be helped unless he or she is ready and willing to be helped. As the old Chinese proverb states, "When the student is ready, the teacher will appear." After learning these great lessons, you will have the urge to share this information with your friends and family, but you must wait until they are ready to receive this message.

It has been usual for men to think and to say, "Many men are slaves because one is an oppressor; let us hate the oppressor." Now, however, there is amongst an increasing few a tendency to reverse this judgment and to say, "One man is an oppressor because many are slaves; let us despise the slaves."

The truth is that oppressor and slave are cooperators in ignorance, and, while seeming to afflict each other, are in reality afflicting themselves. A perfect Knowledge perceives the action of law in the weakness of the oppressed and the misapplied power of the oppressor; a perfect Love, seeing the suffering, which both states entail, condemns neither; a perfect Compassion embraces both oppressor and oppressed.

He who has conquered weakness, and has put away all selfish thoughts, belongs neither to oppressor nor oppressed. He is free.

A man can only rise, conquer, and achieve by lifting up his thoughts. He can only remain weak, and abject, and miserable by refusing to lift up his thoughts.

Could elevating my thoughts really change my life? Is it really that simple? As I pondered these questions, my mentor's voice came into my mind. "Adam," he said, "you have done it your way your entire life. How about doing it my way for once?" At that moment, I made a decision to do things differently. The transformation that I experienced was miraculous. I received an abundance of money, better health, peace, and even better relationships with my wife and family.

Before a man can achieve anything, even in worldly things, he must lift his thoughts above slavish animal indulgence. He may not, in order to succeed, give up all animality and selfishness, by any means; but a portion of it must, at least, be sacrificed. A man whose first thought is bestial indulgence could neither think clearly nor plan methodically; he could not find and develop his latent resources, and would fail in any undertaking. Not having commenced to manfully control his thoughts, he is not in a position to control affairs and to adopt serious responsibilities. He is not fit to act independently and stand alone. But he is limited only by the thoughts which he chooses.

I have known people who have had a lot of money who were not at all spiritual or what we would call "good people." Does this mean that they are successful? Defining success solely on the premise of making a lot of money is a shallow definition of wealth. What about being wealthy in health, relationships, and internal peace? The people who think they are successful without these three vital things are deceiving themselves.

There can be no progress, no achievement without sacrifice, and a man's worldly success will be in the measure that he sacrifices his confused animal thoughts, and fixes his mind on the development of his plans, and the strengthening of his resolution and self-reliance. And the higher he lifts his thoughts, the more manly, upright, and righteous he becomes, the greater will be his success, the more blessed and enduring will be his achievements.

Calm the mind and tap into the higher you, the spiritual you. By doing this, the heavens will conspire to bring success to you in the fastest, most efficient, and most lasting way possible. How can you learn to tap into the higher you? Prayer and meditation are great ways of doing this. It does take some practice. Having a coach help you with this is invaluable.

The universe does not favour the greedy, the dishonest, the vicious, although on the mere surface it may sometimes appear to do so; it helps the honest, the magnanimous, the virtuous. All the great Teachers of the ages have declared this in varying forms, and to prove and know it a man has but to persist in making himself more and more virtuous by lifting up his thoughts.

The wicked and corrupt of this world may prosper for a time, but sooner or later their circumstances are bound to reflect their negative thoughts. A good example of this is Bernie Madoff, who swindled billions of dollars from people and now finds himself serving a life sentence in prison.

Intellectual achievements are the result of thought consecrated to the search for knowledge, or for the beautiful and true in life and nature. Such achievements may be sometimes connected with vanity and ambition, but they are not the outcome of those characteristics; they are the natural outgrowth of long and arduous effort, and of pure and unselfish thoughts.

Spiritual achievements are the consummation of holy aspirations. He who lives constantly in the conception of noble and lofty thoughts, who dwells upon all that is pure and unselfish, will, as surely as the sun reaches its zenith and the moon its full, become wise and noble in character, and rise into a position of influence and blessedness.

Achievement, of whatever kind, is the crown of effort, the diadem of thought. By the aid of self-control, resolution, purity, righteousness, and well-directed thought a man ascends; by the aid of animality, indolence, impurity, corruption, and confusion of thought a man descends.

A man may rise to high success in the world, and even to lofty altitudes in the spiritual realm, and again descend into weakness and wretchedness by allowing arrogant, selfish, and corrupt thoughts to take possession of him.

Victories attained by right thought can only be maintained by watchfulness. Many give way when success is assured, and rapidly fall back into failure.

All achievements, whether in the business, intellectual, or spiritual world, are the result of definitely directed thought, are governed by the same law and are of the same method; the only difference lies in the object of attainment.

He who would accomplish little must sacrifice little; he who would achieve much must sacrifice much; he who would attain highly must sacrifice greatly.

Visions and Ideals

The dreamers are the saviours of the world. As the visible world is sustained by the invisible, so men, through all their trials and sins and sordid vocations, are nourished by the beautiful visions of their solitary dreamers. Humanity cannot forget its dreamers; it cannot let their ideals fade and die; it lives in them; it knows them as the *realities* which it shall one day see and know.

Each creation of man had its birth in an idea. Dreams and imagination are what shapes our world more than the critical mind of man. How do you treat someone when they share their dreams with you? Do you tell them it will never work? Do you tell them they are crazy? All of the greats throughout history were seen at one time or another as being a bit crazy. From the Wright brothers to Columbus, people that have changed our world have dared to dream what was at one time unimaginable. Therefore, encourage the dreamers—help them give life to their dreams.

Composer, sculptor, painter, poet, prophet, sage, these are the makers of the after-world, the architects of heaven. The world is beautiful because they have lived; without them, labouring humanity would perish.

He who cherishes a beautiful vision, a lofty ideal in his heart, will one day realize it. Columbus cherished a vision of another world, and he discovered it; Copernicus fostered the vision of a multiplicity of worlds and a wider universe, and he revealed it; Buddha beheld the vision of a spiritual world of stainless beauty and perfect peace, and he entered into it.

Cherish your visions; cherish your ideals; cherish the music that stirs in your heart, the beauty that forms in your mind, the loveliness that drapes your purest thoughts, for out of them will grow all delightful conditions, all heavenly environment; of these, if you but remain true to them, your world will at last be built.

The greats throughout history have used this power to change the way we see our world. It is powerful to think of the impact that these men have had on all of humanity.

To desire is to obtain; to aspire is to achieve. Shall man's basest desires receive the fullest measure of gratification, and his purest aspirations starve for lack of sustenance? Such is not the Law: such a condition of things can never obtain "ask and receive."

Dream lofty dreams, and as you dream, so shall you become. Your Vision is the promise of what you shall one day be; your Ideal is the prophecy of what you shall at last unveil.

The greatest achievement was at first and for a time a dream. The oak sleeps in the acorn; the bird waits in the egg; and in the highest vision of the soul a waking angel stirs. Dreams are the seedlings of realities.

The great Sequoia is the world's largest living thing. A fully-grown Sequoia tree can grow up to three hundred feet tall. I am amazed as I look at such a small seed and ponder how it can grow into something so magnificent. Our great ideas start out as seemingly insignificant things. As we consistently give faith and belief to our dreams, the powers of heaven respond and miracles come forth.

Your circumstances may be uncongenial, but they shall not long remain so if you but perceive an Ideal and strive to reach it. You cannot travel *within* and stand still *without*. Here is a youth hard pressed by poverty and labour; confined long hours in an unhealthy workshop; unschooled, and lacking all the arts of refinement. But he dreams of better things; he thinks of intelligence, of refinement, of grace and beauty. He conceives of, mentally builds up, an ideal condition of life; the vision of a wider liberty and a larger scope takes possession of him; unrest urges him to action, and he utilizes all his spare time and means, small though they are, to the development of his latent powers and resources. Very soon so altered has his mind become that the workshop can no longer hold him. It has become so out of harmony with his mentality that it falls out of his life as a garment is cast aside, and, with the growth of opportunities which fit the scope of his expanding powers, he passes out of it forever. Years later we see this youth as a full-grown man. We find him a master of certain forces of the mind, which he wields with worldwide influence and almost unequalled power. In his hands he holds the cords of gigantic responsibilities; he speaks, and lo, lives are changed; men and women hang upon his words and remould their characters, and, sunlike, he becomes the fixed and luminous centre round which innumerable destinies revolve. He has realized the Vision of his youth. He has become one with his Ideal.

> *Do not be deceived by mediocre circumstances. When you change within, your outside world must change as well. You cannot stay stuck in a mind that is free from limiting beliefs. Hold on to your vision and your ideals. Believe it until it becomes an obsession. Focus on it with all your heart and mind. Think of your dream every chance you get. Focus all of your energy on your dream with unrelenting persistence. No power in heaven or on earth will hold you back from the fulfillment of your righteous desires. You have greatness already within you. Living the life of your dreams is your birthright as a son or daughter of God.*

And you, too, youthful reader, will realize the Vision (not the idle wish) of your heart, be it base or beautiful, or a mixture of both, for you will always gravitate toward that which you, secretly, most love. Into your hands will be placed the exact results of your own thoughts; you will receive that which you earn; no more, no less.

Whatever your present environment may be, you will fall, remain, or rise with your thoughts, your Vision, your Ideal. You will become as small as your controlling desire; as great as your dominant aspiration. In the beautiful words of Stanton Kirkham Davis, "You may be keeping accounts, and presently you shall walk out of the door that for so long has seemed to you the barrier of your ideals, and shall find yourself before an audience—the pen still behind your ear, the ink stains on your fingers and then and there shall pour out the torrent of your inspiration. You may be driving sheep, and you shall wander to the city bucolic and open-mouthed; shall wander under the intrepid guidance of the spirit into the studio of the master, and after a time he shall say, 'I have nothing more to teach you.' And now you have become the master, who did so recently dream of great things while driving sheep. You shall lay down the saw and the plane to take upon yourself the regeneration of the world."

The thoughtless, the ignorant, and the indolent, seeing only the apparent effects of things and not the things themselves, talk of luck, of fortune and chance. Seeing a man grow rich, they say, "How lucky he is!" Observing another become intellectual, they exclaim, "How highly favoured he is!" And noting the saintly character and wide influence of another, they remark, "How chance aids him at every turn!" They do not see the trials and failures and struggles which these men have voluntarily encountered in order to gain their experience; have no knowledge of the sacrifices they have made, of the undaunted efforts they have put forth, of the faith they have exercised, that they might overcome the apparently insurmountable, and realize the Vision of their heart. They do not know the darkness and the heartaches; they only see the light and joy, and call it "luck." They do not see the long and arduous journey, but only behold the pleasant goal, and call it "good fortune," do not understand the process, but only perceive the result, and call it "chance."

In all human affairs there are efforts, and there are results, and the strength of the effort is the measure of the result. Chance is not.

Gifts, powers, material, intellectual, and spiritual possessions are the fruits of effort; they are thoughts completed, objects accomplished, visions realized.

The Vision that you glorify in your mind, the Ideal that you enthrone in your heart—this you will build your life by, this you will become.

How true this is. As I have worked diligently to improve my mind, people have said that I am just naturally a positive person. As my financial situation has greatly improved, they call it luck. They have not seen the refining process that I had to go through—they see only the gold.

Serenity

Calmness of mind is one of the beautiful jewels of wisdom. It is the result of long and patient effort in self-control. Its presence is an indication of ripened experience, and of a more than ordinary knowledge of the laws and operations of thought.

Having peace of mind is a great indication of where you are in your understanding of the mind. Does it take time and effort to get there? Of course it does. Is it worth it? Yes! In a world where we are constantly bombarded with negative information, it is more important than ever to find that internal peace. Be of good cheer—your mind naturally wants to get you there. You simply must remove the mental and spiritual stumbling blocks.

A man becomes calm in the measure that he understands himself as a thought-evolved being, for such knowledge necessitates the understanding of others as the result of thought, and as he develops a right understanding, and sees more and more clearly the internal relations of things by the action of cause and effect he ceases to fuss and fume and worry and grieve, and remains poised, steadfast, serene.

When you realize that you are the master of your circumstances, all things are possible. There is no need for negativity. Why should a man complain about the food that he himself made? You have a choice to make it better next time.

The calm man, having learned how to govern himself, knows how to adapt himself to others; and they, in turn, reverence his spiritual strength, and feel that they can learn of him and rely upon him. The more tranquil a man becomes, the greater is his success, his influence, his power for good. Even the ordinary trader will find his business prosperity increase as he develops a greater self-control and equanimity, for people will always prefer to deal with a man whose demeanour is strongly equable.

The strong, calm man is always loved and revered. He is like a shade-giving tree in a thirsty land, or a sheltering rock in a storm. Who does not love a tranquil heart, a sweet-tempered, balanced life? It does not matter whether it rains or shines, or what changes come to those possessing these blessings, for they are always sweet, serene, and calm. That exquisite poise of character which we call serenity is the last lesson of culture, the fruitage of the soul. It is precious as wisdom, more to be desired than gold—yea, than even fine gold. How insignificant mere money-seeking looks in comparison with a serene life—a life that dwells in the ocean of Truth, beneath the waves, beyond the reach of tempests, in the Eternal Calm!

Isn't it nice to be around someone who is calm and confident? There is nothing greater than to have internal peace. Everyone has the ability to develop it. It is mankind's natural and balanced state.

How many people we know who sour their lives, who ruin all that is sweet and beautiful by explosive tempers, who destroy their poise of character, and make bad blood! It is a question whether the great majority of people do not ruin their lives and mar their happiness by lack of self-control. How few people we meet in life who are well balanced, who have that exquisite poise which is characteristic of the finished character!

Yes, humanity surges with uncontrolled passion, is tumultuous with ungoverned grief, is blown about by anxiety and doubt only the wise man, only he whose thoughts are controlled and purified, makes the winds and the storms of the soul obey him.

Tempest-tossed souls, wherever ye may be, under whatsoever conditions ye may live, know that in the ocean of life the isles of Blessedness are smiling, and the sunny shore of your ideal awaits your coming. Keep your hand firmly upon the helm of thought. In the bark of your soul reclines the commanding Master; He does but sleep: wake Him. Self-control is strength; Right Thought is mastery; Calmness is power. Say unto your heart, "Peace, be still!"

The wise man has total control over his emotions. The successful person commands his or her emotions and is not subject to them. It is your positive emotions of faith and belief that will activate this power within you to alter your life. You truly are the creator of your life.

> *"People would save so much time if they would stop trying to find themselves and started creating themselves."*
>
> ## Author Unknown

*I have helped thousands of people all over the world get what they want in life, and I can help **you** too! If you want to achieve greater health, wealth, and happiness, and you want it now, visit www.adamsecrets.com.*